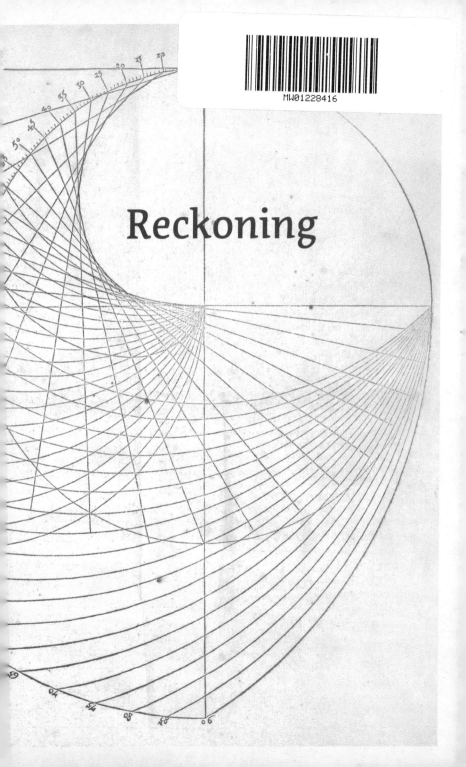

Reckoning

Reckoning

Patrick Friesen

Anvil Press // Vancouver

Library and Archives Canada Cataloguing in Publication

Title: Reckoning / Patrick Friesen.
Names: Friesen, Patrick, 1946- author.
Identifiers: Canadiana 20230221920 |
ISBN 9781772142167 (softcover)
Classification: LCC PS8561.R496 R43 2023 | DDC C811/.54—dc23

Book design: Marijke Friesen
Cover images: Blue and yellow illustration: Shutterstock
Line drawing: Library of Congress / Science Photo Library, "Magnetic dip and latitude. Page from 'De Magnete' (On the Magnet, 1600) by English physicist William Gilbert (1544–1603). This diagram was provided by Gilbert as a means of using a magnet to determine latitude without any need to see the Sun or stars."
Represented in Canada by Publishers Group Canada
Distributed by Raincoast Books

The publisher gratefully acknowledges the financial assistance of the Canada Council for the Arts, the Canada Book Fund, and the Province of British Columbia through the B.C. Arts Council and the Book Publishing Tax Credit.

Anvil Press Publishers Inc.
P.O. Box 3008, Station Terminal
Vancouver, B.C. V6B 3X5 Canada
www.anvilpress.com

PRINTED AND BOUND IN CANADA

In Memory of Margaret Sawatzky Friesen
1926–2020

what shall we do with the drunken sailor?

1.

small in all that blossoming, settled
on a branch in the magnolia, the bird
that sometimes hovers before my face,
eyeball to eyeball, sussing me out,
my large face and big-eyed staring,
the bird perched for a moment in a memory
of blossoms, the slow flow of sap,
an idle moment, a scent, and a return,
until a sudden sideways slip, almost
not a motion at all, the hummingbird
disappearing into the mind of the dream,

that opening,

2.

tag, you're it,

reaching out and touching another
of our species, or avoiding the touch,
chaotic zig-zag running, pell-mell,
as if there's no order in the field,
everyone looking to escape the predator,
screaming, all of us panting and
laughing with the craziness of the
game, the animals that we are,

all the horses run away,

3.

a teenager banging away at that padlocked gate,
when was it closed? who closed it when I wasn't looking?
that door being the only way out of the garden,
that place passing for wild, the precision of rows,
the domestic bliss of order,

but always a momentary escape through falling
blossoms or birdsong, language a child understands,
wordless and worthless, but some kind of ancient
memory, and now a memory of the memory,
like the old woman shelling peas in the back yard,
the woman who reached out and touched my face,

oh yes, I've been shaken by time, grabbed by the collar
and shaken, whatever of it is left, that source of nostalgia,
what slid by, and how do you get out of that impasse?
well, there's always the river,

not the one with the waiting rowboat, I mean that other
oblivion, all memory drowned, how else to explain
my lethargy, drunk on river water, is this where
the return begins? starting over in old age, body
falling apart according to plan, and no blossoming
wisdom, kneeling on the muddy riverbank, thirsty
once again for mind,

4

my spirit must have arrived somewhere, but
I forget where, a town, a street, some
shade beneath a tree, but in this body,

is it the brain that holds things together, gathers
them into a story? grandfather's horses, the pine
and birds, thousands of them crossing the sky every
day, separating them out, heron and passerine,
the owl at night, pulling it all together, humans
attending the cradle, milling about in the kitchen,
or at worship, talking, all that small talk, do you
mind? how are you? yes, yes, and no, holding
it together, assembling and framing, and when
the brain falters the stories skew once more into
something unfamiliar, something from long before
you, and those pieces won't be put together again,
not ever, will they?

and the spirit?

5.

open question, which used to matter, but it's gone
irrelevant, was that the glory? an endless phoenix
fire, or a seed inside a seed inside an immaterial
womb, it's what the brain has drawn together, but
something more,

the bird arriving in the magnolia, waiting for the nearby
montbretia to bloom, waiting for something sweet,
waiting and hovering and vanishing,

that navigation of latitudes and winds, of the scent
of endless gardens, of updrafts and rivers, and the
map of that tiny body,

from matter to mind, a navigation,

6.

ready or not,

hide and seek, but not finding, at night,
you hidden in a hedge as your friends
pass, searching and talking about you,
but you don't exist in that moment of solitude,
as they pass, alone on earth with a chill and
ecstatic freedom, crouched there, detached
from the voices fading into the dark, shivering
with the autumn air rustling among the lilac
leaves, shivering and gazing at a harvest moon
on the horizon, so close in its infinity, and you
are the man on the moon,

here I come,

7.

the story of the farmhouse in flames, the despair
of the man with a pail of water in his hand, his children
sleepy in the grass, watching their lives being shaped,
first the mother dead, then the flames one night,

and the return of horses, their long heads at
the window, looking in, a long age having passed,
and no time at all, a man with the world ringing
in his ears, those flames, those distant flames I never saw
seared in memory, the old woman with the enamel bowl,
the still body in time, her eyes considering the boy,
him remembering marina's seven bell-towers,

and the walls of alhambra, hennaed women walking
in the gardens, by the waters, and someone saying yes,

8.

I am a burning house, I said, almost a question, just
beyond a question, and climbing the stairs into thinking,
bothering into the poem, like this, looking out the window
at people walking their dogs, picking up their shit, and
walking out of the frame of the window into some oblivion,
meaning it happens, move it on, from scene to shining
scene, feeling my way through smoke toward what
must be a door,

9.

metaphors and more metaphors, so slippery, beautiful
lies, evasions, and sometimes all that is possible,
finding a way home, listening to lhasa's *el desierto*,
that raw voice, the meagre terrain which still holds
a song, a nighthawk and laughter in the desert,
and the failure of metaphor,

10.

the misery of rain in january on
a cold sidewalk with a dead flashlight,
where there are no weddings or birthdays,
living in a hole,

how do you sleep?

tents sprout along the harbour,

others are greedy for armageddon, a rage for death,
some with avarice in their pockets, burning fossils and
forests,

us parasites on the face of the earth,

how do we sleep?

11.

More people are huddled in the doorway than are sitting
in pews within. A few are sleeping, one is singing a quirky
dirty song that sounds as if he's making it up on the
spot. None are begging. Everyone knows who they are.
They've been there forever. Everyone knows the ritual
dance; pretending not to see is most popular, there is the
avoidance two-step, and the well-dressed one stops to go
through her purse to find a loonie. An old woman spits
at her patent leather shoes and laughs until her skeletal
body rattles into a tubercular cough. "Beggars," she rasps
breathlessly, "they're all beggars." There are no pigeons
about; they're off, casing the Bulk Barn. Always moving,
agile in their hunger.

12.

audacity, one of them and not one of them, a boy
kicking the table with his rattlesnake shoes, looking

for some buried ritual, something that must have been lost
or misplaced, all those hours swaying in the tree, finding
words and song and finding a key, the audacity of a boy
knowing his direction, and folding the map,

getting out of place into another story,

breathing free in the foliage, unknown, and willing
to be unknown, a wandering mind,

I can show you says the boy,
the old man asking *can you hear me?*

13.

tired tulips, ruffled glads, the bicycle bell, well,
all of it, the shambles of a mind, father and mother
in the ground, and conception that first act of dying,

crows, pampas grass, humans, on and on, the dead
boy, ah there's a beginning, a fool for time, an inexorable
extinction, can't say it better for the moment,

14.

an arthritic knee and at the root of a thumb, well let's
not bother with a list, leave decay to the imagination,
but my eyes turn toward death more, today I wonder
what eyes will be looking at my face, me lying supine,
a nurse, or perhaps the kind face of sister irene, after
all the thousands of faces, it may come down to some
stranger by my bed,

or on some road, some sidewalk, or beneath a table as hav
dryly puts it, medics at my clothes and pulse,

15.

stepping into the bone dance, flayed skin and sinew,
this water change, this last change, I must, I must change,

the man who kept losing hair year after year until he arrived
at what he was supposed to look like, another baby,

death is minor, like birth or baptism, like marriage or
    graduation,
another earthly moment, another disappearance,

charles elliott shaves a felled cedar, soothing the grain
    with his hand,
working it to where tree and artist meet, becoming
    each other,

the last visit to the graveyard is not to learn, but to sing,
to leave behind a consolation,

16.

the swifts above the cathedral in seville, descending
thousands of feet, navigate with clarity through dusk
and into night, skimming around spires and the giralda,
dark emissaries of the dark past, all that has not been
accounted for,

17.

dogs howled at the moment the sun died, the town eclipsed,
almost lit, almost not, and the man said that I must pray for
forgiveness, and for what I asked, I haven't murdered the sun,
and he said it isn't funny, but of course it was, the man holding
his bible against my forehead, as if my head was porous,
mangling some language, and those great secular bodies
kept rolling through all that vastness, and birds were silent,
just for a moment, and the world hushed except for the man's
uncertain tears as he pushed me out of his car and drove into
the sun's profane rebirth, I had no direction, only a way,

18.

Interpreters. Storytellers. Gods and trees. And so, what?

19.

When did homo sapiens first sing? Was it a phrase, a long
line, a song? Where was it, in an open field, the top of a tree,
beside a fire, where? How was this singing heard? Did the
listeners become still? Were they in thrall to this new sound,
this series of sounds? Or, had it made its way gradually from
a few notes, to a phrase, to a song over time so that no one
paid attention?

Why?

20.

the clatter of knives being washed at the sink, my mother
singing as usual, and I shift from the real world to the open
window above the sink, and out, some bend of time,
a transfer, a kindling, the sun flaring around the world
and nothing more,

yes, that woman and her song, what I would take in and
leave, the window she opened, her clear blue eyes gazing
into mine,

21.

waking early, slowly, moving from dream to memory,
that haze, and then awake to another generation,
another era, one I don't belong in, one that has changed
its habits, or rather has brought new ones to baffle
mine, and I must change but not to those rituals and
stratagems, I remember too much, I remember what
made me, the faithful body that grew me, the birthdays
with sandwiches beneath the sugar trees, a careful foot
over foot walk along a rail fence, the buried ones, yes,
I remember words that were spoken by many, so
many, words that did not reveal what was meant,

well, strangers already, receding memories touching
each other and shaping themselves into story,

a ghost story,

22.

coming to words, secretly reading comics in the basement,
or unseen in tall grass, gazing at passing clouds, and then
silence for a moment, the cosmos all around, and earth
going on,

the calendar with its divisions, sun and moon,

what words can only hint at, time, and forgetting,
perhaps the most important part of memory, what is
unrecalled, but known,

turning from culture toward horticulture, well not really
that, nothing invented and maintained, just soil which
keeps becoming,

23.

me, a walleyed fish, swimming beneath the full
moon's reflection, through the streets and cul-
de-sacs of the lit underwater city, *lili marlene*
beneath a lamp post and, humming *marble halls,*
the irish tenor strolls along the canal grande back
to nora, and away from the lights, on some back
street, a familiar woman from long ago who sings
me to sleep,

24.

a sparrow dust-bathing on the path outside my
window, life upon life, them parasites choking,

delicate feathers swiftly rearranged, and in their
infinite parabolas swallows dip distant waters,

and motion, always the motion from cell to cell,
sparking synapses, one foot after another, the erratic
mind of a crow heading home to roost, my mind at
work, and love, and fear, and the hummingbird
in still air,

an ancient shoeless human watching the sparrow,

and me on the tidal flat digging for clams and afterbirth,
story after story, and never finding the first, a mind
waking beneath the sea,

25.

my bike was writing me through town paths and
alleys, writing me along town line road toward
african trees and the sand pit, gliding my sturdy
hiawatha into the land of reverie,

later came the words,
by my own hand,

26.

becoming word-glutted in a scramble to unravel the non-
sense of the child, astonished now at what didn't need
unraveling to begin with, blackbird and marsh, that
immediacy,

the colour of dusk, the smell of the sugar maple where
the heretic lived for seven years with the only question,
listening to the breeze among the leaves,

clovis points and mastodon bones, and before that, ages
and more ages,

and climbing down, lingering, unsaved as usual,
standing beneath the porch light, inside mortality,

27.

the landscape where I played, and lay
in the grass, or watched birds in the marsh,
the roads and walls above that landscape,
above lost trails, forgotten trails, the way
through the bush, across rivers, what passed
before grandfather's barn, his few cows,
the fences and haystack, traces of a narrow
trail, overgrown, and those who walked there
now dead,

the singing there was, and dance,

there are those who sing their way
through the landscape, and there are
birds that sing to their eggs, like women
to their wombs, singing spirit out of
water,

28.

squelching my way through a living marsh, tussock
to tussock, among red-winged blackbirds singing
and circling as they rise from reeds, me finding an
island of wrecked cars, looking for one with
a live battery and a radio, flicking stations to
find rock 'n' roll,

almost hearing them birds thirty-thousand
years ago, you know? like I was there, like
the world was just starting, but it wasn't,

1959, me sitting on torn upholstery, no doors,
dried-out wipers scraping across the window,
music floating me into some future, me
coughing with the smoke of stolen cigarettes,

alive you could say, truly, but so what, just
another summer day of the dead,

extinction becomes us, our stupidity
in this little infinity, this planet in its weathers,

29.

and there's the hummingbird at the lucifer montbretia,
a slight breeze waving them both in late afternoon light,
suspension in motion, that's hardly it, don't know the
language, using this one instead, and that's it, why any
of this nonsense, human gall and drive, me alive within
some idiotic gift, sitting stunned inside the beauty,

the unbearable velocity of the hummingbird's heart,

30.

from the top of the maple I could see
the steeple and the pine tree beside it,
an orientation, and a navigation, thinking
of broken bodies, coming to that, all
the broken bodies,

and the mind, the infinite mind gone to earth,

31.

there is a clearing that watched her many times
walking the perimeter or still on a bench, waiting
for a deer which is watching her, unseen from
a thicket across the clearing, and she observes
the field, she hears birds, though not the deer
which makes its slow way among trees, around
the clearing, and arrives behind the bench where
it stands, watching her, until a third eye opens
and she sees, she knows, and is glad,

she no longer dreamed the rowboat where her
dead husband waited, his arm calling her, at least
for forty years she ceased that dreaming,

there is a clearing, and there was a woman who
was a child, there is a clearing, but the mother
is gone,

32.

history with the usual fictions threading
it all together, our stories cross-stitched,
what I didn't know of hers and she couldn't
know of mine, but I'm remembering how she
named me and I decided I must be irish,
the tin whistle that could make you believe
in nostalgia, and me an adopted boy, finding
my way toward dedalus and molly bloom,
toward the drunken tenor in a bar, and
the welshman, and all the other voices, toward
the place where anything can happen,

my own clearing,

drinking the blood-red wine,

33.

this is how it happens, a stuffed cloud
comes apart above the back yard, now,
the distant cylinder of a plane glints
in the sunlight, seven white calla blossoms,
a japanese maple,

and nothing, nothing but that,

34.

a brown-suited man
standing with a hymnal

in his hands,

his head turned slightly
to read the words with
his good eye,

a man, a father, singing
baritone harmony,

it was,
wasn't it?

maybe 1956, one
sunday, one moment,

a man without doubt
in the words he sang,
though so much doubt
in himself,

a child in the pew beside him
tracing ancient maps in the book,

the man carrying what no one remembers,

35.

A hairpin falling to the floor, her hair undone, and
nothing the same again, so the story goes.

The story the man told, over the years, the story he
heard of his young mother drowning in her lungs, and
calling, terrified, the room turning, and someone closing

the blinds to keep something out, perhaps the rooster at
dawn. This is what was remembered in all the agitation; it
was November 1918, and him becoming an orphan.

A dog barked all night, that too was remembered, though
it had nothing to do with anything.

36.

my darlings, my children, our years
together, the anxieties and laughter,
music and dance, the finding and
the forgetting,

that's how to love, to see what
is there and no further, my children
have seen me as eve has, their love
looking at me from many distances,

and I saw my father from a lone distance,
taking the few words he offered that told me nothing,
until I learned to hear the orphan, all that stirred
between the words,

37.

where there's only one door
to your room you need to understand
it well, when there's a radio
in your room you need to wait
for the right song,

always the waiting is nearly over,
which is why it takes so long, why
you never get there,

it was words first came between us,
words that could take me anywhere
he hadn't been, him

born into his language, and me borne
out of it, how do you travel between
languages?

and I kept a slovenly garden,

38.

what we did was laugh, a way of staying loose,
snickering behind our hands in church, ralph and me,

breathe on me breath of God, and us thinking
halitosis, being teenagers and the corpus making
itself known, laughing ourselves loony,

how else to break the padlock for the day
when we'd be gone for good, and us breaking
from camouflage, in different directions,

raw talk and dancing in the apartment,
all of us clowns on cheap wine beer
and hash, not to mention freedom and
blasphemy,

it was the laugh of acquittal,

sweet hour of darkness, and the danger
of some nights,

hildebrand, besotted in his basement, with exacto
blade in hand, etching a print, and me watching
beneath the light bulb, watching until the light
burned out,

39.

finding spinoza and tillich,
but what did I know? a young
mind unraveling what had
been knitted for me, all loose
strands and frayed ends,
a prisoner to words but growing
averse to knitted things, the itch
of them, slipping into an
unsettling conversation, now
and then,

40.

swimming out of the past,
a fishbone caught in my throat,

41.

a pedlar, a knocker on doors, and reading camus,
smoke rising from his broken car, a brief incense
drifting over that decade, all-night talking,

first at the pub, then my grimy apartment,
sisyphus and the guillotine, and life without
creeds, that embrace,

with *testimony of the rose*, with *broken english,*
I recognize the lifelong poem of the body,
margie moves like thinking, you know? image
image image,

what her body remembers of the bodies going
back millennia, the body always between
places, glimpsed in a gesture, an act of theatre,
of moving atoms, like brask finding motion
in the latent body, moving the actor in that
stillness, himself a mind dancer,

42.

a brief history of letting go, again and
again, sometimes unknowing, sometimes
dejected, becoming an age your children
see from a distance, you have left selves
behind, selves you remember and align
within the story even as you disengage,
is this the freedom you haven't found?

and coming, perhaps, to molly bloom,
to the word, saying it uncertainly, but
saying it,

43.

do you see me? my daughter, my son,
do you still see me? I am your father,
what does that mean? my father let go
everything slowly, then abruptly, and
he became no one,

he returned one night as no one,
waking me to the spinning fire he was,
I remember how mother called him lover
on his last breath, now it was his farewell
to this wayward son, to our small lives
mingling for a moment in a vastness,
sharing a kitchen table, a garden, and
inadequate conversations, disobedience,
and then the room was empty, and no one there,

if you listen you can hear the whirr of
its wings, a blur, the hummingbird
pinned to the sky,

44.

roaming, finding my way on the highways,
walking the shoulders, thumb out, waiting
for the next vehicle, making up songs by
singing them aloud, picked up by vw vans
and impalas, remembering a radio jacked
up high on canned heat singing wilbert harrison,
a couple of minutes, a couple of hours, what
do they matter in a lifetime?

or riding the grey goose between town and city,
between histories, and through histories,
riding through some novel that I thought
I knew, a novel without a plot, and me gazing
out the window at the passing land, learning
it is a land of spirits and burials, a land of murders
and disappearances, a land where you can
still hear drums,

navigations,

let's work together he sings, and it was
the 60s, I travel differently now, I notice
the mile signs, and the horizon is not distant,

45.

There may be nothing after death; I tend toward that.

Or, everything. But I doubt it.

Someone singing through an open window. This I know.

46.

the man in the blue baseball cap was laughing it up
in the mortuary, but he was brought to his knees,
still laughing because there was nothing else to do,
laid low by the jitters, and the flaw in his eyes,

he was a dervish in his room, dancing vertical
to a horizontal song, going airborne when he lost

restraint, ah that's the way with these songs,

he ditched the map he was given, walls shaking
with the radio blasting, and he knew how
he was going,

47.

I don't sleep so well in the summer, it's the light,
the heat of day warming into night,
I throw covers off, moving between seasons,
each one a recurring revelation, always new,
always primal, and each summer I long for
rain,

and rain comes, the lowering sky and green
smell, what the dead will never know again,
and me still here, lethargic with heat, watering
peonies calla lilies and wind flowers,

and tell me is freedom what you were born from,
or what you die toward?

the complexities of love, each one and kind, and
despair, all that electricity coursing through
your body, a grapple with it, or growing
old, your love waking beside you, touching
you, all night you dreamed you were awake,
and you wonder that this will end,

you remember heat hallucinations when
you were a child, the world gone dark with
synapse flashes on the inside of your eyelids,

and you prone on the sidewalk, in another
world as if you walked into a cave of drawings,
dots and dashes beneath your eyelids, and you
are primitive and phantom, your mother with
her hand on your shoulder rousing you back
into time,

when there's freedom, if that's what you think
it is, you're always coming from it or walking
toward it, you know?

listen, I chose for myself to be something
or nothing, whichever it came to, I was
no more free than that, but it seems there
is something between,

48.

dickinson walked up and down the stairs, between
the kitchen and her room, between callers
and the brief visitation of the poem,

there was that navigation, a lonely one, but a sure
one that no one knew, and she arrived where the
horses were headed,

49.

macewen's eyes were dark stones
with the fullness of the earth in them,
like the *fallen eyes of angels*, with
everything they'd seen of mystery

and doubt, her still walking down bloor,
looking for the secret room, at least
that's how it seems some days, such
intensity doesn't vanish quickly, it
leaves an aura behind, or a faint pillar
of light,

50.

there are rivers to cross,

it's an old song, sing it,

a lament for maria, carried past
a window on the shoulders of
four men, on the way to her grave,

sing it for the child she suckled
on her death bed in 1918,

a mother, but already a grandmother
long before grandchildren were born,
and none of us remembering her,

sing it for

anna in her passion, caught
in the river, the woman who
gave birth to a grandfather,
her only child,

my grandfather, with a player's plain
between his fingers, never revealing

the secret of the river, but telling stories,

crossing rivers, the rat, red, the seine,
and always a last river, watching it flow
out of time,

sing it, *row row row your boat,*

51.

Swimming is surviving in water, all that flailing and
gulping. Why put myself through that? I'd rather be
near it, feel a breeze coming off it, or on certain nights
at Patricia Beach, no one within miles, squatting in Lake
Winnipeg, with a full moon painting a path toward me.
After a while I wonder if I'm painting that path toward
the moon.

52.

I may well be in a car driving toward death, Sigmund, but
I'm sitting in the back seat, and I don't see anyone at the
wheel. It's a 1946 model. Mostly the view is good, even
astonishing at times, though the car has been speeding up
lately, and the landscape flashes by a little faster.

53.

P: Two rhinos meet on the banks of a swift-flowing river.
   One rhino says to the other: "why do I keep thinking
   it's Thursday?"

G: What river was it?

P: Irrelevant.

G: OK, but finish it.

P: That's all.

G: But what's the answer?

P: No answer.

G: So, what's the joke?

P: You get it or you don't.

G: Do you see me laughing?

P: Each day being the only day.

G: No idea what you mean, and why are you laughing?
   Are you laughing at me?

P: Give it time.

54.

not either/or, but between, or rather both,
juggling yes and no from hand to hand,
maybe, wanting nothing more than that,

living between, along the arc of a nijinsky
leap, that hanging arc, which is now,

the poem of the body, a step, silent
hands, an aging face, the absence
between steps,

55.

I heard the drum at the cellar jazz club
talking, and I listened like it was taking
over, *let's get lost*, or it was distant,
drifting through trees, the drum singing
as it has forever, a drum, a hand, and time,

56.

red hands on cathedral doors, *departed*,
is that the word? it was, but now it's *disappeared*,
a red hand across a mouth,

57.

Twenty thousand years ago, standing at the mouth of
a Spanish cave, did someone, at twilight, comment on
the beauty of the light? Or, thirty thousand years ago
at Chauvet or El Castillo, or earlier in Indonesia, or
South Africa, did someone rise in the morning, saying it
was going to be a lovely day? Did someone, a hundred
thousand years ago, stop to enjoy the flow and shape of
cumulus clouds?

58.

the heat will do us in, the forests of the world
ablaze, our lethargy turned to panic, the species
unsustainable, exhausted with denial,

as a dog returns to its vomit,

our slow deaths become sudden, and that mirage
of a lone distant figure walking in the desert is not
some saviour but a remnant, flayed by heat,

59.

the kid I was, walking that line, like a wallenda,
falling often, returning to the solitude of my sea-green
room, the radio cranked on the holy palaver
of *tutti frutti*, and don't give a rip of *twist and
shout*, becoming free in a way, in that small
room, dancing into the walls, a recognition
of what was, at the moment, what the dervish
was, not so much what he was born into but
where he was born from, unknown and making
himself known and never getting there, bantering
on the street, on the page, in the hall, mocking
his way to the grave,

and moments, you know? moments to break
the banter, like love, grief, or the hummingbird,

recognition,

something small before the void,

60.

anna, it may have begun with her,
anna with mischief and secrets in her body,
me watching her funeral procession, her
coming apart in that dark hearse,

on stage nepinak bringing anna alive
with words, at least as alive as a life in death,

and redekop in toronto speaking the words
of another wild woman, saying it's all play,
always has been as the child knows, and
look over there, a clown behind the tree,

nagle in winnipeg, shattered, her fine
shattering, that fragile face, and her living
in the minds of others, coming to an end
of so much electricity,

all of this, fable and myth, inside us from
the beginning of sense and thought, how
the earth moved us, and we began the thread
of song, unknown beneath our painted faces,

61.

fully-clothed she descended
the staircase, somehow losing her clothes
on a landing halfway down, which
is where I greeted her, all motion slowing
to a kiss,

and that was motion, only now is it
memory, or the idea of it,

us meeting in a house I no longer remember
except for the stairs, how I got there and
how I came away, there were clothes scattered
on descending steps,

it was motion, you know, because time passed,

62.

the footprints I left on a snowy field,
a rabbit's line, that zig zag track
escaping the wolf, and the road, that
beeline, on the way somewhere, but
really nowhere, walking the river's
bank, the bend of the flow, now the
sea, arriving at the sea, all the paths
converging, finding my way by pulse,

63.

emerging from sleep, having already
forgotten dreams, a wind arrived
during the night, you think you heard
it, blustery, though it might have been
in a dream, this morning it's ruffling
water in the harbour, you're looking
at the list you wrote last evening,
caught between remembering and forgetting,
and what you need to do to be human,

turning your face to the weather,

64.

and the cities we live in, you can hear
their bones crack, you can feel ligaments
stretched to their limits, sun shining off
tree-top leaves, people slouched in the
shade, and an empty bus with a "not in
service" sign the only movement,

there are rumours of fires approaching,
surrounded by dried-out forests, a cigarette,
lightning, even a spark from a passing
train, not much is needed now to light
the tinder of our lives, even some godly
wish, there is so much rage in the arid fields
and streets, all the beliefs that release death
on the world,

the buried ones will return, an old
woman, in her absolute stillness,
dances a welcome,

and the bony dead in this room
where nothing happens,

65.

in sixty meters turn left on catherine street,
I've come to know that voice, no larynx,
no vocal cords, not even a breath, and I read

how people lose their way sometimes with
this voice, mostly old people it seems, those
who still remember stopping to ask directions,
perhaps on the corner of mary and skinner,
or thirteen mile corner let's say, or some place
where only a song will do, where there are
no phones, well, that's going too far,

losing your way, bewildered, and moving on,
past that dead birch, angling right toward the
shimmering aspen, do you remember?

and finding your way,

remembering back alley shortcuts, and town line
road leading to africa, or old tom road, across
the creek, your tinny transistor hanging from
handle bars, the animals singing *bring it on home
    to me,*

and you're in another world, of music, of imagined
cities, a world much older than you,

*in six meters turn left, and you will have arrived
    at your death,*

66.

I have become the slack-assed old man I used to watch
at the gym, four decades past, not doddery yet,
but living inside someone's ancient skin, wondering
where I've been,

I have tracked an animal all my life, following
its spoor, moving between foot and mind, getting
close but never more than glimpses at night,
moonlit eyes in a thicket, and nothing there
at first light but scat,

lost in my age until I find the track again,

and learning how quickly the weather can turn,
out there in the places I walk through, and in
here,

I am fortunate to have been lazy,

67.

there are stuttering angels that come to speech,
clear and drunk, almost still in that fusion, a motion
that cannot be measured or weighed,

but I don't know, there must be other ways
to say that, or not,

not say anything at all, it comes to that,

and yes there were moments of fearlessness,

68.

A bird fell out of the sky, frozen in flight. That was
the winter no snow fell, and the ground was iron. I
was reading The *Rime of the Ancient Mariner* and

thinking about my father. My ancestry seemed to
have disappeared. I couldn't trace it past my great-
grandparents, and I knew nothing about them. It was all
a blank as if they had abruptly appeared on earth two
hundred years ago. *Ex nihilo*. I have recurring dreams of
flying. I'm high above the earth, drifting, looking down
on the diminutive towns and roads. Suddenly I'm falling,
plummeting. A moment later I smell the earth, loam and
forest. One of these times I won't wake. That same cold
winter I saw a frozen gull on the roof, its feet caught
beneath a shingle, wings wide-spread. An appalling angel.

69.

the evidence of time, palm prints
along our way, and still the unanswered
questions among fish and shin bones,
in the spirit still there in the caves,
and in the footprints of a mother
and child,

and what is our story now?

70.

them frogs are leaving, won't know them soon,
disappeared down warm rivers to some cove
of lost things, the bear turning away, bones
of her cubs lying in the blanched field,

us too, thinned out through heat and rising rivers,
and vanishing, it will come to pass, yes by our own

hands, a trawler on its side in the desert, or cities
disappearing beneath waters,

71.

carrying fair margaret across the north sea in wintry weather,
the ship foundering, and only the hat of the sailor,
sir patrick spens, left floating, and arising from beneath it
a song come alive, becoming sir patrick by dead reckoning, a
wonderous navigation,

and another, *idea* the learned man said, something to
believe, and I thought *idol*, but we all believed more
ardently, *idle*, I said, finding my voice, and still they believed,
it was a dead-end navigation, the wreckage of the good ship
carried onto wild shores,

72.

returning to lhasa often, *el desierto*, a dusky voice on fire
with love lost, singing that she had a place on earth,
calling for something hidden in each of us, percussion
banging at the door,

73.

is that belief in her voice? a voice
that seeks but never finds, lucília
do carmo singing the story of the
redeemed whore, *maria madalena*,
the woman they feared, the body

that could take them anywhere, and
maybe it did,

that voice, the guitars, could make
me almost believe anything, the story
adrift in history, in the singing the song
becoming something else, caught
between belief and passion,

74.

the only revered body the crucified one,
sing it, *ave verum corpus*, the beauty
of the song, the celestial voices, like
the ballerina *en pointe*, almost un-
earthly, longing to leave this planet,

75.

about time, someone said, meaning they had run
out of patience, but I was thinking it might mean
a much bigger thing where impatience has no meaning,
but I forget what came after that,

out of time is what it's come to now, closer to the end
than to the middle, but also something about the journey,
what we emerged from, creatures that we were
on that arm-dangling simian path,

it is about time, that drip drip of seconds that takes
no time at all, and who remembers? us critters

vanishing with a last word or two of comfort or
conciliation, or perhaps only a silence broken by
traffic, or a nurse fiddling with an iv, yes, it's all
about time, something to unearth, always
to unearth it,

76.

barefoot in a small town, the kid who stepped on
a nail, a lynchpin of civilization, his grandmother
wrapping a poultice of sour cream around the wound,

and him, with his foot raised to a chair, not fully awake
from a thousand wombs ago, before nails and chairs,
who knows what scraps and threads are stranded in his
brain, some memory emerging as a dream, a stray image,
frayed at the edges, a moment's flash,

and there he is laughing in church, that passage
from sober to guffaw, no stars lighting the way,
just the flow of a mind

happy in its blasphemous life,

77.

remember the boy in his unknowing? not
diminishing into certainty, alive with shifting
words, the sounds of them, accepting fact
as magic, a trick of the mind, the eye deceived
into knowing, conceived again,

a boy in the shade of a tree, thinking *I exist,
so I must exist*, and laughing at himself
and all the facts,

and the tree a mother,

I am, so I am becoming,

conceived,

78.

there's mischief, yeah, all the way
to the cemetery, mischief in my
blood, going back, the mischief of
anna, the old woman with rascal
in her eyes and work in her hands,

riffing in the back yard, mother
hanging up the wash, her words
flying into songs, and me hearing
without listening, riffing into my
own stories, into the mischief of
topsy-turvy,

walking into church backwards,
let's say, letting the wild soul out
to forage,

79.

What I heard was *the monk observing his vowels*. I
imagined a chapel with rosy light from high windows
crossing a stone floor, the monk chanting, air entering his
mouth, down the trachea to his lungs, and then back out
again. A kind of hallucinatory poem, that repetitive cycle
of air shaped by its passage into Gregorian song. I saw the
oblong O of his mouth. Like the mouth of a dying man.
I've seen that, and I've known that long, last exhalation
of breath. That abandonment. Like William Blake singing
hymns as he died, his joyful mouth open as a vowel. His
breath released like a vow.

80.

how to take in all the buried children, and the implements
of colonizers, those ruthless gardeners, or rather
to take it in but not find a place for it, because
there is no place for it,

81.

the species abhorrent, us, in our cruelty
and stupidity, working our way toward
extinction, but what to say in all this
prosperity and starvation, the vacancy,
eating donuts and praising god, and
so much malice,

in the face of endlessly circling one star
within a million stars, everything being true,
you just have to laugh,

82.

S: You've never been there, you have no past in Dublin.

Pádraig: I do. I've walked through the snow to Michael
    Furey's grave.

S: But there's no Michael Furey.

Pádraig: Ah, but there is. I remember him.

S: It's just a story.

Pádraig: Yes, it is.

83.

rising through a deep-sea sleep I shaped
my life, remembered and dreamed it into
story, though some directions no longer
exist, episodes are in disorder, but somewhere
in all the chapters something happened,
I know it, though nothing happened in chapters,

the tale is out of time, almost out of time,
and will be adjourned,

84.

remembering the thread of a story until it frays
into an image, someone turning her head, but
who? a glance and a blurred gesture at the periphery
of vision, coming out of memory, bringing nothing
with me, breaching into moonlight on sand,
my hands stranded like starfish on the duvet,

85.

I have known other landscapes, imagined ones
that I moved through like maps, tabakova and joyce,
for example, a goya etching, mullions and transoms,
moving through what I see or hear, what I smell,
turning at a bend in the road when stephen dedalus
stopped on a bridge to watch a young woman knee-deep
in the river, coming to a clearing when I heard *spiegel
im spiegel*, or much earlier when the green radio
blew open with *I saw her standing there,*

the horizon from the top of a sugar tree, how infinite
and how near, me chewing the node of a lilac stem,
remember the days of us children knowing our way
by dream from the first watery place, and then walking
into memory?

and what era are we in? what came a hundred years ago,
fifty, ten? how do we locate ourselves?

trees and barefoot paths, they are burning, and
homes are smoke, what now?

86.

Flat-out in the dentist's chair, gazing at holes in the ceiling
tiles, and the hygienist asking me questions I can't answer
because her hands are in my mouth. Thinking back to the
Reformation, or just after, when the people I come from
came into being, and trying to imagine how different they
were just a few years earlier? Was it just a matter of a year
or two and then that immense distance they travelled?
Away from Rome for one thing. She touches a tender spot
and I wince. She asks me what I'll be doing this summer,
but I still can't answer. In this case, I also don't know,
summer being a distance that has changed since I was a
child. My father was born on a desolate farm, still he had
straight white teeth and a good smile. The hygienist takes
her hands out of my mouth but has no more questions. I
feel lucky.

87.

well, she said, *I remember*, and she meant
let me tell you a story, and I listened and said
that's not exactly how you told it before,
and she said *of course not, you were younger
with different ears, so which one is true,
or at least truer?* and she said *yes*,

88.

wiping sweat from her brow with
a forearm and looking around at
her garden, she was happy,

though a sudden grief sometimes
arrived, the grief of love, and
there was a sorrow children bring,
she was working out her time and never
living less,

standing still in a loose shirt, the hoe
leaning against her shoulder, she
loved what her body knew, and
what it lost,

89.

you take the high road and
I'll take the low road

ach, she sang her way to scotland,
not arriving, the song going on,

like richard manuel's hobo jumping
a ride toward a vanishing point, and

me working my days, a shovel across
my shoulder, filling the holes I dug
on the way here, then

it gets to tramping, to hell with work,
gets to lowering my ass to the ground,
motionless, still finding a note or two
to sing,

that poverty,

she did take the high road, finally
arriving, arrived afore me, ach,

90.

she left stories I didn't know
I remembered, she held my
childhood there, and I have
been visiting, not to find that
child but her, the teller of stories,
the one who rejoiced on earth,

remembering how she spread
the blanket for my birthday picnic,
the blanket holding everything,

91.

the door to the room was ajar,
just enough to slide through, the room
lit by red kaffir lilies in a tall glass vase
on top of the piano,

where I played my clumsy music,
my first music, the sugar tree just
outside the picture window, and
me caught between that room
and the tree,

leaving and returning, always
sliding sidewise through that door,
ajar,

92.

There is distance in disbelief, between reality and story.
I believe it, even if it's one step. Feeling my way, not
arriving, almost lost. Still holding that first journey, the
nine-month distance within, the noise of it, song and
clamour, light and water, oh yes utterly lost in that first
place.

And something happens, things begin to happen, so
autobiography begins, dove-tailing into that unutterably
long story that never began.

In and out the back door, lilac shrubs and raspberry
canes, a creek, a dirt road, finding my way by foot,
running, and then lying flat on my back in tall grass,
gazing at that distance. Earthling.

93.

that sepia flicker of memory,
an old film, all light and twilight,
the darkness from which
we surfaced,

the tick-tock of it, the oscillation,

where memory disappears, and
reappears, always vanishing into
story,

remembering the recent dead,
and the ancient, forgetting,

94.

a cough across a mile of fields,
quarter moon etched on a winter
night, and a figure in the cemetery
clearing snow from a headstone with
a gloved hand,

the prairie has hardened so many,
and buried them, you understand
things coldly on such nights, not
much room for sentiment, and
too much for love,

thinking of a scar in the air
where someone has walked out,

thinking of the meaning
we scramble for within
meaninglessness, well,

not for long,

and there is no scar in the sky,
only in you,

95.

that's not me, not the old man in the
barber chair with an opinion, the sound
of scissors at his ear, he has no opinion,

glancing at the mirror with its dark corners,

how much is that doggie in the window?

96.

Another story, one of several nearly-identical ones. I don't remember where it came from. It is a story of settlers and their horses on the prairies in winter. A man, a distant ancestor, has taken his horses and a sled many miles to another town for a visit. A blizzard threatens so the man leaves for home, but the snow arrives fast, and he's in the midst of it. Night is falling. Soon there is no visibility at all. Knowing something about his horses, the man holds the reins loosely and lets them move forward on their own; they know the way home. They plod for hours, the weather getting colder, and so they vanish into the night. In the morning, a woman looks out the window and sees the horses standing in the back yard. Inside the sled sits her frozen husband. He took the long way.

97.

nothing sacred about songs or words,
no scriptures there, just moments of transition,
profane blessings, spirits in the flesh, rope-walking
between earth and stars,

eve, absolutely still, leaning forward,
fingers motionless on the keyboard,
her eyes staring the words into extinction,
until they finally come alive,

the topography of mind, finding a way

into the poem, naming what the feet touch,
the mouth saying the babel of the mind, all
those sounds we've made,

working at night when distance diminishes,
listening to the sound of rain, and you clear
your throat,

let it rain,

98.

us frightened sapiens, blind with anxiety, filled
with rumors of peril and uncertainty, on streets,
in towns and back yards, hemmed in and becoming
inhuman, penned children gazing at their hands,
agile thumbs and the loneliness of excess in the face
of starvation,

what do you say? carrying it all in your body,
and wandering in your mind, what can you
say?

there was fearless laughter, there was, and
there was disarray in the face of order,

like the abyss the dead leave behind,
or the field of a glance across a room,
like a clear day on the prairies, space
filled with time,

so we tell tales to get a handle,

99.

aye, that's the story, and it's nothing
but evidence, true or not, all of us in this ship
of mirrors, the perfect camouflage, now
we're here, now we're not, light shifting
from hour to hour, and we're sailing
without a captain, just us denizens,
aye aye,

100.

so what, that slow build, then a minute and a half into
the track jimmy cobb's crash and chambers walking
his bass into the cellar, that moment when you're seized
by the collar and you enter a place called time, or
rather you don't move at all,

101.

listening to a poem read slowly, waiting for the leap,
that hard-earned leap, but beyond work, looking easy
as bichette, and it arrives, reminding you once more
how the mind leaves a person and looks back at them,

so what,
it's nothing, an emptiness,
a demolition, and then
breaking open,

this too will be lost, and that you regret,
that last beautiful *so what,*

102.

a life braced by doubt and the small fundamental
certainties, birth and death, and cats are not
the only ones to hallucinate their way through
this tiny existence,

103.

standing up to hear a voice singing
in some backyard, to see the only cloud
in the sky slowly losing its shape, thinning
into wisps and then nothing, damp sheets
on the wash line, the unthinking joy of
the child whirling round and round and
the old woman passing by, laughing
at the sight, swept by body memory,

which one is rejoicing?

104.

sam the magician, with a fortune-telling
clock, has neighbourhood kids under
a spell in the back yard, and he's made
it snow in august, and the parents are
nostalgic for belief, even if it's disappearing
coins or good will surfacing in the world
again, and I'm the man in the doorway
not believing in magic, only its mechanics,
the how of it, the way sam's hands move,

the way he talks to distract, and always
the sudden pleasure of the accomplished trick,
no magic in that, only that I can't work it out,

some things vanish only to return, like a coin
or the three of clubs, other things simply vanish,

105.

there are memories that cannot fit the story,
they are too hard-edged and won't be shaped,
simply not malleable, no suppleness to them,
an overheated room in the church basement,
or a dark suit in a black car beckoning, stones
on the road of a narrative, adding nothing but
fear, and who wants to die afraid?

these were persistent insinuating voices,
which entered the story anyway but have
been knocked about through time, becoming
shards, weapons for a while, then flints to
light a fire, all embers now, not to be breathed
on too often, or ever again, the old grumble,

where is this going? the story too smooth perhaps,
even for old feet, doors slowly closing, one by one,
only the gate to the boneyard remains, where the tale
will be bound into a book of invisible ink,

it's going nowhere, like all knitting, coming apart
in time, and is it true that there is a clearing
where everything happened? and me sunburned

and alive, yes, that's it,

and a red dress I remember,

106.

a wedding dress, and love,
the nearest word to it, a barefoot
love finding my hand,

107.

yes, we walk in circles,
isn't that what lost people do?

until they're found,

108.

there are people who can't stop singing,
like pete seeger, like my mother who sang
while she worked or walked, shaping her
breath she sang out of sorrow and into
joy, it was nature, first impulse, a heartbeat
in the world, arriving from the planets, from
deep earth, imagine them gazing at a white
moon and raising song, long ago, imagine
their dance, feet creased with dirt, and
everyone singing,

growing up with that sound, a clear
soprano, and her and father harmonizing
as they washed dishes, her voice after
he was long gone becoming trembly with
time, and then husky, but on the note,

still shaping her breath,

109.

me listening to *inside looking out*, hearing
burdon's breath, the way it drops to a rasp
after *canvas bags*, the muffled pulse of
the bass drum, almost tachycardic, and
a release, those *thoughts of freedom*,
learning how to breathe words from inside
the body, finding out,

110.

there was music from the fire, she said,
watching a roma encampment from the trees,
where had they come from with a music
she'd never heard before, a sound scorned
and held at bay, their raw guitars untuned,
their voices strange and high or, in town,
were their ears open at all?

she crept closer to the fire, feeling its heat,
and no one seeing her as she opened her throat
to the unearthly vibration of earth,

that was a story she loved to tell, how she
moved from the sleeping town to the fire,
and returned with a song,

a voice singing within the silent explosion
of the universe,

III.

the division of days, and their naming,
tgif, freya's day, or the hush of sunday,
thursday, it always feels like thursday,
keeping track like strokes on a cell wall,
minutes and hours, an order in all the
immensity, some kid licking his rainbow
ice cream, and there's darkness on the land,
the moon turning away,

112.

the smallest seed of a galaxy opening
in a nanosecond, spreading its debris to create
time and space, and us, us, were we born
out of a million years of rain? barren rock
holding the sea, our mother, were we?

113.

returning, a fluttering fall into the sunken city,
the womb opening and closing, swimming again through
mother, pausing for a moment to rest, at a café table

perhaps, to mull things over, reckoning, dead reckoning,
the story so far, and how long it's taken, almost not
a story at all, but time and how it has moved, the motion
of a mind through a body, a leaf falling past a window,
at least that's the way it seems, and I don't know better,

114.

crack of a bat, you turn and burn,
seeking location, tracking, then leaving
earth, flat-out, midair, you catch the ball
white as an ice cream cone in your black
leather glove, and you know how your
body exists in the world,

there is no theology here, only a perfect
motion to remember all your life,

115.

Nathalie Léger is watching baseball on a television
screen, half-listening to a man anxiously talking about
the ruins of Holy Land, an American Christian theme
park they've just visited. He thinks ruins are witness to
illusion coming to an inevitable end, though he prefers to
talk about the profits the park made at one time. Léger
wonders how something as small as a baseball moving
at great speed can be hit by a stick. It is the aesthetic of
precise motion in a second that causes her wonder. And
she will wonder, soon, about Pippa Bacca, a performance
artist, hitchhiking from Italy toward Jerusalem in a white
wedding gown as a hopeful gesture toward peace. She

would not change her dress, said Bacca, or clean it, till she
arrived. There is naivety in goodness, and there is carnage
in creeds. Somewhere, having crossed the Bosphorus, the
bride was stripped of her stained bridal gown, raped and
strangled, well short of Jerusalem.

116.

the wonder of disappearance, in
a forest or desert, from one room
to another, or death, the moment
absence begins, one morning you
hear the coffee grinder, you see
a clear sky out the back door, next
morning you don't,

you don't know what happened,
that's left to the coroner or to some
holy one who doesn't know they're
holy,

117.

look into the simple mirror and see
no wisdom, only a blue-eyed spirit,
and a wintry moon, well that or
nothing, that too lies in the mirror,
what things we discover, what things
we devise to soothe the spirit, what
cradle songs we sing,

118.

Is there a word for what I feel? Have I forgotten it, or do
I need another language, one that holds the exact word?
One that knows? Another language, another face. My
mind looking through the window at me. The memories
I hold in my hands, in my feet, memories that never got
as far as my brain. The memories of fear locked in my
shoulders. Words behind closed doors or from the pulpit.
And learning to redeem language, its rhythms and sounds,
embracing words for their ambiguity. Such a relief. Then
burning all the flawed maps on New Year's Eve, fire in an
enamel bowl in the snow, that ritual.

119.

is nature mother or
mothered? of earth,
that spinning clump,
out of the darkness
of her, out of night and
shadows,

digging, not flying, finding
a way back to what looks
like origin, but is only a deep
watery distance,
what mothers hold, that
distance, and for nine months
the most intimate voyage,

and the waking cry, a pivot
from sea to sun, an arrival into
fierce splendour,

120.

out of microbial waters,
photosynthesis, ferns and sugars,
out of sunlight on *the face
of the deep*,

aeons of motion, of cells and
swamp, the smell of foliage
and decay, and always

mothers, carrying the seeds,

a mother, briefly, between there
and there, alive in earth's details,
the touch and sound, the relentless
on and on of it, the sorrow, her
skiing across a white field beneath
a full moon, the earth she loved,
and what no one remembers after all,

but something's left behind, a flotsam
of words, *girl, menno, laughter, curiosity,*
words on *the face of the deep*, before
they sink, like all words, that slow
unnaming

into photosynthesis,

121.

sung into being, vibrations through
the walls of the womb, mother earth

singing, mother singing, and that
rock steady, four-four heartbeat,
a knocking heard through the cosmos,

ah, with so much culture there is
barely room for wonder, but that
hardly says it when you are the son
of the mother, is that what I mean?
where you are suddenly empty with
what you see and hear, with scent,
with taste and what you touch, all
of it, so that they disappear into
recognition, *tjanne* in my child's
dialect, yes something like that,

and my mother finding herself in
some story, sitting on the top step of
the porch, and me in the tree watching
her, and father rounding the corner
with long strides, coming home from
work, whistling, that's it, my human world,
seeing it through for a moment,

122.

a song on the radio, and you think of
a friend or relative who is long dead,
the music woven into that memory
igniting it, lighting the only place
a person lives after death, or animal,
or a garden one day one summer,
you can feel the heat on your back,

peas in your cupped hands, a place
inside a song,

the shorter your remaining
days, the longer your story, a shadow
lengthening behind you,

ah, soft, try not to stoop to
the nostalgia of your own life,
leave that to others as they enter
the life you leave behind, or rather
forget it,

here now, that's you, motherless
and fatherless, an ancient orphan
today, which will become nostalgia
if you let it, the story more important
than now,

123.

a skittering call of gulls across
the water,

is nature the first language,
the unspoken language from which
all words are born?

I mean the silence before gulls,
if it's even possible to fathom that,

an unfinished mind wandering,
wondering, a micro microcosm,

imagining the grinding machinery
of one random galaxy, just the one
is enough for now,

124.

I used to imagine an edge past which there was
no going, where earth and abyss met, a place
which was an end of me, where the flying buttresses
of thought crumbled, and you never found them
dead birds,

125.

it is night as tugs manoeuver a barge
loaded with crushed cars over the reflection
of the streets, darting flashlights reveal
workers moving among steeples of
metal, their thin voices above the
deep throb of engines, it's an image
of nightmare, the lead tug's brilliant
light suddenly shining on me at the
end of its watery path,

to digress: the underwater city, glittering
beneath the barge, may be the only repository
of democracy, the baptized city of the drowned,
from here to there, in the dark,

126.

With liquid nitrogen the dermatologist burns a basal
cell carcinoma from my scalp. It feels like I'm doing
time, and perhaps I'll get out one day. The Lord willing
says the doctor, a master of clichés he believes he
understands. And I'm thinking, out in the sun. I know it's
too comfortable inside. But are all discomforts good for
your soul, or are they all equally good? Well, never mind.
There's really no comfort anyway though sometimes
I think there is. And when does ritual become habit?
Remembering the nuns in St. Boniface floating down
Taché in their grey habits. I wondered if I'd ever get out
of the fifties. I began wondering that about every decade,
and I always got out but just as far as the next one. The
sun burning its way into my skin, deeper each year. The
immensity of distances. I'm tired and don't bother parting
the curtains. It's about time.

127.

the so-called vibration of the universe
may simply be a gigantic ungodly snore
of sleep,

dream away saints and sinners,

128.

Olivia: Because we reproduce ourselves, and because we
    live in a limited space, there can be no endless time for
    us human objects.

Anna: I'm not sure … I mean, you're not talking about
    eternity, are you?

Olivia: Endless time, not eternity.

Anna: There's a difference?

Olivia: Time is our world. And we must end time, each of
    us in our own time.

Anna: Death. OK, making room.

Olivia: And we have at least two kinds of time. Motion
    and stillness. Imagine a moving car. It tells a story in
    its motion through space and time, the story moving
    steadily ahead. But the front passenger opens the
    glove compartment, and time stops right there. He
    finds things, like a flashlight, a bag of wipes for a
    baby, a tin box of sweets, and other things. That small
    compartment is a still moment as he sees these things
    and thinks about them. He lives in stopped time,
    without dying. It is the intersection of horizontal and
    vertical, the narrative and the poetic, at the same time.

Anna: Not exactly scientific.

Olivia: Exactly.

129.

distant and not, standing outside a house,
looking in at the window where your children
and grandchildren are laughing and talking,

busy with details you've left behind, or
forgotten, or never knew to begin with,
and thinking that maybe fraud charges
won't be laid at your feet, perhaps one
advantage of age, a kind of sympathy that
ages you even more, and you step back
from the window, your reaching hand still
touching the glass,

and what is that animal you keep tracking,
though the trail is broken now, and you
navigate by memory, that flawed device,
you no longer hear traffic from a nearby
highway, or a phone ringing, there's just
this goad in you, this useless momentum,
and, well,

there are truths which are not facts, you
make your way toward them and sometimes
you live with them, but these words don't
get there,

what you have is stamina, those threads
that hold your life together, but

as usual you trail off, and the ache remains,
love,

130.

it was a soprano gave birth to me,
singing me into my name, a voice
I don't hear anymore, a disappearance

I understand but don't believe, how
can one be born to a voice and stay
borne when it has vanished?

unmoored,

for a moment but then finding my voice
again, raspier now than it was at the first
separation, still singing that song planted
in the child's throat,

a song of questions and resilience, what I
thought was freedom, though it didn't matter
what it was called, making my way is what
it's called,

131.

some are born to loyalty, others to betrayal,
I was born to both, and I was a lazy kid in a
worker's world, there are no marxist tears
in these eyes, it's song over slogan, no altar
calls or sermons, no flags, no anthems either,

I was a spitfire for a time, wanted to pull down
the factory pillars, but who was I? in that anger
who was I?

not much of a song here, not a lot of
paradise in my eyes, a juggler I was,

132.

a hummingbird on a barbed wire fence, and
you remember a dirt road and a distant figure
approaching, an old woman who stopped
before you, and you halted, trying to read
her beautiful hands, the world suddenly alive
within her silent gestures,

133.

a dream of birds, a redwing on its reed,
what it means isn't clear, it is what it's
always been, a soul, a word that means
little on its own, but when it's swaying
in a breeze you know enough, and you
recall it often, a reverie of black feathers
shining in the still heat of an afternoon, a
long interval, breaking then into a simple
moment, the bird trilling solo, a song from
a hidden world, a lucidity in the marsh,

134.

A: Have you ever touched the naked back of a woman
     without feeling desire?

John: What do you mean by desire?

A: Desire. You know? Wanting to make love to her.

John: Touching the bare back of a woman without wanting to make love? Why did you reach for her back in the first place?

A: Wanting to touch beauty, especially the beauty of someone you love. Sliding your fingers down her spine.

John: So, wanting. That's desire, even if it's an aesthetic want.

A: But more …

John: More is desire.

A: More than beauty, more than form; it's touching the skin of one you love. Something outside of need. Knowing one day you will not be able to touch that skin. The skin is love, even when it's old, touching it, knowing it. It's what we are for a second. You wish you could memorize that touch. Not desire, but irrevocable loss.

John: Maybe you'll die first.

A: Maybe she memorized my fingers on her back. Memory, you know. It happens when you're not looking.

John: What a lovely cliché. And you think memory tells the truth?

A: No. But it tells a story.

John: Soon to be forgotten.

A: Or changed.

John: True.

135.

turning in my sleep, and yet not fully
asleep, aware I'm turning, like a lull
in the dream, unaware on both sides
of turning, and me half-awake in the dark,
born like all others to grow into extinction,
wondering about all that disappears
with each death, stories, stories, stories,

some passed on, shifting, evading, telling
some truth, now and then, others are fiction
only, and most are forgotten, it's a slippery
rehearsal, and what do I know for sure?

moments or words or gestures, nothing
memorized, but coming back to me un-
intended, set off by a song or a passing
storm, and there it is, a forgotten story,
hiding for years behind a curtain, and
what life has it lived silently in my mind,
what shaping as I worked or loved,
did it slide into memory,

waiting to be sparked?

136.

memento, he said, meaning
momento, standing at the harbour
in trieste, picking up a flat stone,
saying joyce used to swim here
with his son, he was remembering
a passage from the novel, but
that was another life, other waters,

and him living another memory,
momento, and skipping the stone
out to sea, watching four splashes,
then nothing,

like the seasons, he thought, though
he wasn't really thinking, turning
back into the city,

momentum,

into streets he'd only read about,
momentum into some past he remembered
where he turned the page but kept returning
to the passage that was joyce's memory,
becoming his own,

on edmonton street across from central park,
where old men played chess in a young world,
though it was long past,

137.

collapsing mind, one day, like any solar system
collapses, unable to hold together, returning
to random,

is that a question?

memories frayed, or grown, all finally
undone, the knitting unravelling into
a spidery chaos on the floor,

138.

what the body can take of abuse, from
the mob, some random assailant, or
a teacher, what the body can take
of the knife, of fist and nails, of the
thrown stone, the strap,

and what we do to our own bodies,
the flagellant in his cell chastening his
back with a whip, or the pulpit's scold
against pleasure, no kiss is holy, the
body's desire an affliction,

the cutter in the bathroom, spirit
caught inside the numb flesh, a flick
of a blade, such a short distance, opening
the body like a flower to its pain,

anger or joy, what pain covers,
a scourge against being, as if there is

more to it than that, as if there is a
separation that we must widen, is
that the meaning?

139.

let me tell you one thing, but wait,
I've forgotten, there are too many
things flickering in my brain,

worn
thoughts, images

skittering,

like stones across water, and
they sink,

140.

the momentary concentration of a
hummingbird, not a physicist drilling
through strata of thought toward
an impossible beginning, where the
hallucination of numbers is a longing

that ends in ashes,

earth spinning, the milky way spinning
and no still point, just the music of wings
fluttering by,

is that the metaphor? it's been used,

141.

The mind is a map that can show you the direction to
anywhere, to some Assyrian battle, for example, to a
Canaanite encampment, or to the deep snow where
ancient wolves tracked caribou. You can still hear
them howl, that call hanging on air. And us, almost
unimaginable beings, emerging, always emerging.
Everything in motion.

Even cave paintings change. Sealed up, lost to human
memory, fading into migration. And the hunt going on,
wolves creeping ever nearer the fire. You can trace it in
your mind, the way things begin to look the way they
sound. The letters, the wolf becoming dog, woof woof,
and the migrant alphabet.

142.

to make a way through the mind,
even as it disintegrates, cell by cell,
a mind of tangents banging at the circle,
a claustrophobia of webs, to find
a way back to the skinny child, born
in a thunderstorm from a thousand
ghosts, but in 1946 from a young
woman, it's what I remember,

her at the piano, my door open to
a sliver of light darkening the room,
lulling me between awake and sleep,
a memory being born, sound, light,

and a slender shadow bending toward the keys,

and love,

143.

it flares bright as an after-image,
and fades away, this last picture
I have of her, shrunken into herself
in the broda, gazing out the window,
she says, *it all goes by so quickly*, and
looking back at me, *inside I'm still 10,*

you know?

144.

from there to there, a girl grows old, a boy,
but then, like all lost beings, coming around
again, awkward

hands and voices,

a late reminder,

: and I was wondering, like a kid, about
time before the beginning, you know?

145.

Denotations. I've grown too old for that though lately
I've almost come to see everything in a gravestone. Those
lives. Talk about reduction. How else to articulate the
inarticulate? And so, disbelieving absence which is almost
an anguish. Not belief, or words, but stone.

A stone, in a field of stones, holding the haunt. The way
the universe keeps expanding. How it fits into a grave.
But that's too grandiose, isn't it? And dubious. There's
nothing there, is there? Nothing but turned soil. Ancient
disturbances.

Standing among the rocks on Dallas Beach, I don't know
what I'm talking about anymore, or thinking. I watch it
all leaving on the tide, like bladderwrack.

146.

how to make room, to empty god and
enter, like stepping into a vacant hall,
a silent hall, until sound drifts in from
behind tired curtains, a confession, like
tabakova's longing cello, and what
endures

            between two gestures, *ma*,
tadashi edo making his way, step by
half-step, along a slick of water on stage,
suddenly twisting and thrashing to the
floor, bruising his body into emptiness,

and those cello notes bending down,
thinking into earth, yes, that longing
for the sacred which is not sacred at all,
but dust swept out of the hall, a fly
knocking against a window, and the
cellist rehearsing outside the door,

147.

Memento, I said, meaning momento, standing at the
harbour in Trieste, picking up a flat stone, thinking
Joyce used to swim here before the Great War. I was
remembering the passage where Stephen Dedalus stands
on a bridge, gazing at the girl in the water, and she glances
back. Did their eyes meet? But that was another life, and
me living another memory.

Momento, un momento, and skipping the stone out
to sea, watching four splashes and then nothing as it
sank. Like the seasons, I thought, though I wasn't really
thinking, turning back into the city. Momentum into the
streets I'd only read about, momentum into some past
I remembered anyway. The Canal Grande and outside
the city, Duino Castle. Turning the page, but pausing
and returning to the passage which was Joyce's memory,
becoming mine on Edmonton Street across from Central
Park where old men played chess, and me waiting for
a seat. 1966. *Tomorrow Never Knows* and *The Circle
Game*. Didn't know everything had already happened.

That summer I stood on the Midtown Bridge in the City
of Bridges; it was early evening. That's how I remember
it just now, standing there gazing at the Assiniboine, a

moment on Earth. That's all, but it keeps coming back to
me, the bridge, the passage. Places I've been, times.

148.

living this biography, what's left out or
unremembered, this biography with its impiety
and refusal, with its euphoria and music,
its rupture of speech, and the familial
laying on of hands, those hands that have lost
their weight, that have lost the world,

149.

tabakova's *radiant*, that climb up
the stairs and a door flying open
to a distant burning prairie sunset,

grief is long and holds astonishment,
that place where comprehension can be
gone through but disbelieved, you know
she has died but she lives, and all the
dualities of the mind can live together,
be true at the same moment, until the body
is encountered, you feel how the radiance
of the live soul has moved from the body
into the air, and the air around the body
gleams with charisma for a short time,
the fire inside the body has left through
every pore, every exit point, and before
vanishing, it enshrouds the flesh with aura,
just for a while, glowing, radiant so you

can't believe absence, but the glow pales
and recedes, then suddenly nothing, just
as you're listening to the absent heartbeat,
and feeling a chill, and you are astonied,

tabakova moves you within the room,
the fire of that cello movement has scorched
the walls, the hair, the hands, and has risen
you to that opening door where the sun
has burned out and is sending a last laser
into your body, the cold flight of an arrow,
and suddenly you understand how absence
itself can disappear, though it lingers behind
things, the lamp on a side table, light turned
on, behind a bookcase, or the cut flowers
straight-backed in a vase, and the lingering
is not long for the pragmatic one who is removing
dead flowers, turning off the light and asking
people to leave, and peggy lee's cello knits
beauty together again briefly, seizing stitches from
the air and knitting them into grief,

150.

there are magnitudes on the ocean floor, our home is not
still, this place we have made home, gasping and crawling
out of the sea,

there is winter rain outside the window, but beneath
the forest floor embers are seeding the coming summer's
conflagrations,

our ships are burning too, the air filled with smoke,
but there are bedtime stories to tell, and always there are
lullabies,

the interrogator smokes a cigarette in the basement,
listening, for a moment, to the cries from other rooms,
he's writing a letter to God,

at the intersection, standing on the curb, someone
hands out tracts, sometimes love cannot be separated
from anger,

151.

rain coming down all night and etta james
crying *like a rainy day*, a voice from the deep,
annie lennox singing *september in the rain*,

a tenderness within the husky voice, and lhasa,
where do these voices come from? two with
a lifetime to build those voices, the other passing
through, like some angel on her deathbed,

152.

Her head is low to the keyboard, a fall of hair over one
eye. Lerner plays through some genetic story. Among the
changes of tempo, the turns and detours, I hear familiar
sounds, what I thought I'd left and my leaving. Music
is a window. I see a figure behind the drapes. A deer
at the edge of a clearing. I see a wintry road beneath
moonlight. I remember someone sang about moonlight

shining through the trees. And music is a mirror. There's not much to say about that. The last chord sustains and Lerner straightens to full posture. It's the way she can disappear and return, her fingers translating, and us breathing inside that transition, it's that conjury I love.

153.

Who remembers before the playground? Distant mirages, us planets floating through the milky way. Hearing that beat, the heartbeat inside, and voices from the other side of a taut skin. Mother holding one hand beneath her swollen belly and singing some old folk song from her schooldays. Do I remember this? Was I already remembering what was to come?

Streaked with vernix, swimming toward that first breath I cannot remember. The shock of it. The gulp of it. A door opening at the end of a hall, and all that sound, that light. Squeezed and pummelled toward it. Drummed and sung into the world.

Can't tell memory from dream sometimes. The child, barefooted, walked along a dirt road in summer heat. Do my feet remember that?

What is held in the cries on the playground? Bodies exulting in motion, or bodies in pain from a fall, all of what it means, all of what it is. The body alive. And how much we forget of that moment as we grow into months, years, and decades, as we divide time. Carrying the hidden child with us.

And the playground. I thought I'd left it behind. But
there's Goya's old man on a swing; you can hear the
ropes squeak. He's practically a skull, but he doesn't care.
Monkey bars and dreaming.

154.

A man is memorizing poems on his deathbed. There's
one by Auden, an Emily Dickinson, of course some
Shakespeare sonnets, but he keeps returning to a poem
by Yeats. All day he sleeps, at night he can be heard
murmuring the poems, a line of light beneath the door.
Where does he think he's carrying these poems to?
Sometimes he takes on the voices in the Yeats poem of
Crazy Jane and the bishop. A small drama on his narrow
bed. Something to remind him of earth. An unholy
passport.

155.

an old woman is walking in the heat, she is
not walking toward an oasis, they have all
dried out, she is looking for the last tree,
carrying the mind of the species to the end
of the earth,

156.

A greybeard was pedaling hard against the wind,
ballooning garbage bags attached to handle bars and
seat. As he passed, I called out on a whim, "where are

you going?" He didn't answer, kept pedaling, his shoes
worn through, his muddy pantlegs held by bicycle clips.
I was wondering how he could afford a high-end bike,
never mind the helmet he was wearing. I was thinking
about where he might have come from, we're all born
somewhere, we're all children, and wondering about all
the detritus he'd picked up and why was he collecting it.
Carrying the ruins of a city in a way. How did he get to
this point? He stopped suddenly, glancing back over his
shoulder and, pointing ahead, he shouted, "do you want
to come along?" He laughed as he turned and pushed
down on the pedals, the bags clinking against each other.
The future, I thought, and ran after him, laughing as well.

157.

some pick huckleberries, some pluck stars from the sky,
what's the difference? the season, our brief bodies are
burning cattails with blackbirds rising like smoke,

always indecipherable, the vastness of a sky with its
million detonations, unnoticed disappearances,

and us moving through it all, what is glimpsed in the
corner of the eye, an augenblick, some detail, an icelandic
poppy, or another life walking by,

and we walk, like kierkegaard through the streets of
copenhagen, mulling his morning's work, thoreau
sauntering perpetually toward some holy land,

like dickinson walking up and down the stairs,
between the kitchen and her room, between
conversation and a brief visitation of the poem,

and we walk like virginia woolf gathering stones on her
way to the river, a long walk to the river ouse,

and the ones who walk at night, insomniacs and the
anxious, pausing in bus shelters to get out of the rain,

a woman I know crosses the blue bridge, seeking
some elusive phrase or finite word, and when
the word arrives she keeps walking, a spill of joy
through her body, she walks further, leaving
the bridge behind,

there is infinity in those shoes, in the long miles, in the bend,
a man looking for the place where night is buried,

158.

I watched the old woman remembering … it wasn't
coming, or when it did was coming slantwise … ages
running into each other … the timing off … she'd drift
away from the story … like smoke …

It's a tangle, like all stories …

She remembered the train … a dream passing …
swallowed by fog … nothing left but that muffled
rumble … and silence …

And a call … a voice from where? … from another
room … that door, I thought I had closed it … my hand
on the brass knob … I left it behind, but yes the door
remained ajar … those voices and all the years …

159.

where will we be when meaning ends,
us, each of us, where?

slippers at the door, drawn drapes,
that kind of evidence, a fallen shawl, or
watching

crow's feet on the skylight, slipping
as it clambers and slides, scratching and
scraping, charlie chaplin with dark wings,
not the angel spoken of,

the interrupted nap,

it's what happens old man,
it's what happens,

a last syllable,

160.

looking back through my children's eyes,
through rain running down the window,
wind in the magnolia tree, looking back
through the scrawny heron in shallow water,
through the ancestor I am becoming, looking
back from the water,

161.

throw it away, sang abbey
lincoln, throw it all away,

162.

drifting through a mirage, then another,
and another, and waking in the doldrums
of dead night, to that ringing silence of
the dying world, tangled in that web
of anxiety, wide awake on a bed, in a city,
a country, on this planet sailing through
an infinite silence, revolving in its momentum
through billions of years, and evolving
relentlessly,

sometimes I come to myself when I close
my eyes and imagine our ancestors, their
bone flutes and cave drawings, the way
they might have sounded, their language,
how they spoke and worked things out,

what they knew and we don't,

163.

memories float away, or slip behind
pillars of habit, but still not letting go,
that last release, the building coming
down, but something stirring in the
rubble,

and then that silent deer appears from
nowhere, an appearance and the world
fills like a silent carnival, thoughts I grow
in my head, what my senses take in,
and breathing deep, amazed that
this deer appeared, and that I shall
not see it again,

164.

milk of first love, a taste on
the tongue which learns to speak,
which learns to love words, and
coming around again, an old man
and the milk of last love, living
by the sea,

the child I was, floating through
the amniotic waters, almost human,
a planet coming to birth, existence
we call it, and all those arbitrary
others, mothers, fathers, and the
whole mystery of ancestry, where
do they come from? where have
they gone? and me astonished
with wonder at the brief time,
passing time with those I loved,
ones I knew, even strangers glimpsed
in some doorway or sky train,

what I saw become an absence,

does it mean something, anything
at all, does the story point somewhere,
or is it only an anecdote within the
roiling larger stories, meaning only
what it has come to, that vanishing
point on the horizon, where it drops
off the end of the earth?

a landscape, a mother and father,
the consequences of them, a maple
sugar to climb, a skin that doesn't like sun
in a land of light, a stand-up piano
and a screen door, that's all and there's
more, much more, me passing by
the details, and them forgetting me,

does it mean anything more than what it is?

165.

those hands are only remembered now,
the voice too, her speaking a dialect
from elsewhere, and me not listening,
but I heard, the child taking in the words,
songs and gestures, remembering,
waiting for a rediscovery, or ad-libbing
in another place another time,
a momentary association out of the blue,
shaping it whole, all of it a rack of clouds,

166.

A redwing rises from bulrushes and flutters silently above
my head. I can't see it as it hovers between me and the
blinding sun. The shadow, though, leads, and I begin to
foot it lightly. I know where I am.

167.

joyce made an angel fart and turned
the sea to snot, crazy jane taught
a bishop that the seat of orgasm
is adjacent to the *place of excrement,*
so close but still a journey, making
our way through that dialogue, like
prayer or copulation, the mechanics of it,
the *how?* and the body as alive as
any ghost, awkward or lithe doesn't
matter, a taper burning down and
snuffed,

168.

laughter, mocking or wanton,
laughter is a moment going on
and on until a prophet holds up
his hand, calling for a belief
that inevitably collapses at the sound of mirth,

submitting to nothing but
earth and sky, no story tells
the beginning but the body,

169.

the doom of old age,
a dismantling,

thumb,

knee,

a hand, both hands,

and memory, yes, clumsy
on the stairs, all thumbs,

did I say forgetting?

170.

holding the baby's bare foot, that unbelievably
soft skin, the hand's mind remembering,

171.

withering, looking down the length of his body
in the bath, red moles sprouting, a bruise on the shinbone,
trying to remember a scar he had for decades,
but unable to locate it, faded now, another story
forgotten, easy to imagine lying in a box about
to be incinerated, leaving next to nothing
for the anthropologists,

light on his feet,

into the dark,

it's nothing,

172.

waking at the same moment, we turn
toward each other and laugh, I begin
to say something but can't find a word,
so I think of the meaning I want and
walk through the alphabet to see which
letter will trigger the word, she does
the same she says, often, and we wonder
how many words we've lost or displaced,
how many more are wandering near
the edge of a clearing, soon to enter that
scraggly bush, and thinking of the dread
of wordlessness, or deranged sounds and
forgotten names,

will we keep laughing? another
word for love,

crazy love, ha,

sing it,

173.

put him in the longboat till he gets sober,

174.

P: That's really weird.

P: Yeah? What?

P: I just had déjà vu.

P: Oh yeah, it happens. What was it?

P: I had déjà vu about having had déjà vu.

P. That's interesting. It's probably happened before.

P: You think? The déjà vu I just had a déjà vu about was a déjà vu about a previous déjà vu.

P: Wow. So, that's what? Three déjà vu's? About déjá vu.

P: It won't happen again.

P: I thought you'd say that.

175.

another ship sailing,

land ho!

well, maybe, maybe
not,

wind blowing my hat away,

all hands on deck,

oh baby,

what a wonder

Acknowledgements

Andreas Schroeder and Sharon Oddie Brown for their great generosity and friendship. Also, Patricia and Terence Young for theirs. Thanks to Sister Irene Rioux.

Per Brask, Magdalene Redekop, and Allan Safarik, for our wide-ranging, on-going conversations.

Several sections of this poem have been put to music, composed and produced by Niko Friesen (David Sikula, mixer and engineer and Brock MacFarlane, mastering). They have appeared on an album entitled *O'Keeffe Bones* and are available on streaming sites like Bandcamp and iTunes.

Acknowledging visual artists whose work has had an impact on me these past few years, and sometimes longer: Charles Elliott, Eva Fritsch, Floyd Joseph, Marianne Nicholson, Dylan Thomas, Esther Warkov, and Eva Wynand.

Thanks to Marijke Friesen for her wonderful cover designs; they speak for the books before they're opened, including this one.

Thanks for the work and pleasure sparked by recording collaborations with composer, instrumentalist and producer Niko Friesen.

Always grateful for the editing and advice of Eve Joseph, and the conversations of a lifetime. Thank you, they'll go on past us.

And thanks to Brian Kaufman, Karen Green and Jessica Key at Anvil Press for taking this manuscript on, and for being so easy and productive to work with.

Welcoming Alíla7 to our family.

Remembering Charles Elliott (TEMOSE<u>N</u>) and Steven Heighton.

PATRICK FRIESEN has published more than a dozen books of poetry, a book of essays, stage and radio plays, and has co-translated, with Per Brask, five books of Danish poetry, including *Frayed Opus for Strings & Wind Instruments* by Ulrikka Gernes. Most recently he has released the collaborative CD, *O'Keeffe Bones*, with Niko Friesen, and *Outlasting the Weather: Selected & New Poems, 1994–2020*, published by Anvil Press.